T0359667

GIRLS LIKE ME

Also by Teri Louise Kelly:

Sex, Knives & Bouillabaisse (Memoir) Wakefield Press 2008

Last Bed On Earth (Memoir) Wakefield Press 2009

Works included in this volume have been
previously published in/on:

Masque

Spin

The Poetry Warrior

The Independent Weekly

Ditch

Counterexample Poetics

Radio Adelaide

Outlaw Press

Moronic Ox

Angelfire

GIRLS LIKE ME

Teri Louise Kelly

Wakefield
Press

Wakefield Press
1 The Parade West
Kent Town
South Australia 5067
www.wakefieldpress.com.au

First published 2009

Cover art: From an original painting by
Teri Louise Kelly & Recyclopath
Typeset by Wakefield Press
Printed and bound by Griffin Digital, Adelaide

ISBN 978 1 86254 868 8

Government
of South Australia

Arts SA

This project Is proudly supported by the
Richard Llewellyn Arts & Disability Trust.

This book is dedicated to

JULIA

(the kind of editor a girl like me needs)

The publication of this book was made possible by a grant from the Richard Llewellyn Arts and Disability Trust and the assistance and support of Wakefield Press. My thanks to them for their continued support of South Australian artists.

The following also need to be thanked for their involvement in this project:

Me
Insomniacal Maniac
Andrew Shaw
Katherine Cummings
Daniel Clarke
Amy K. McDonald
Sue Webb
Scott McGuinness
Georgia Gowing
Michael Bollen
Recyclopath
Amelia Walker
Kerryn Tredrea
Jenny Toune
The Punk Pink Poet
Hunter S. Thompson
My Psychiatrist
Jane Lomax-Smith

Julia Beaven
Sara Branham
Christine Trummer
Justin Lee Brown-Gagnon
Scott-Mitchell Patrick
Kathryn Carmody
Katrina Fox
Alyce Shenntal
Catherine Kenneally
Maria Pallotta-Chiarolli
Shanan Cummings
Kylie Cowling
Merryn Johns
Eva Grzelak
Angela Tolley
My Mother
Lois Lane
Marilyn Manson

Contents

Body Bags & Toe Tags (1999)

in the most
extreme of cases
forensics
yellow tape
latex gloves
plastic slippers
face masks
lines
i got a toe tag
& a zip up
body bag
to go home to my
mum in
economy class
poste resante
par avian
reversed charged
called my bluff
collect
DOA.

No Introduction Required (1959)

You know my name
&
you gave me
the identifying number,
&
so said
John McVicar
&
I agree.

the night before my execution (2009)

all appeals denied,
all stays overruled,
all words said,
all tears cried,
all the lies underlined in red for no redemption
                  i'm thinking i might have missed

out on a point
or theorem
or serum by not getting joyce,
fitzgerald
even mailer
though thankful i got bukowski

        & orwell & you can't get them all right?

& the priest comes & asks me to confess & seek the forgiveness
    of his god thing
                  i decline
                  no time for theologicals
                  no get out of jail card
                  in a stacked deck

i read some of ham on rye again
the sun doesn't rise
only sets
as the clock ticks & the metronome counts the beats
left
& the juice goes on – the tender kiss of volts & they come noisily
    & i wish i'd chosen the italian not the thai last night
one final dice with spice
but the indigestion cure awaits

i see walls
floors, lines,
too much white light

& they ask for my last words
& i can think of thousands
though finally i choose
the most appropriate
& i say, in a clear voice 'the end full stop'

Ode To Luiz #2 (2007)

On his first night in borstal
after the cold shower & buzz cut
Luiz was summarily frog-marched
down to the canteen.

Waiting in a line of rat-faced boys,
Luiz was accosted by a larger, uglier, meaner toad,
and the toad said to Luiz
"I'll see you later tosspot."

Luiz, never one to turn a rosy cheek,
took another stale bread roll
and said to the larger, uglier, meaner toad:
"I can't wait."

The toad, irate, turned on Luiz and scowled:
"What? Are you stupid? Watcha in here for anyhow,
buggery of your neighbour's labrador or what?"
Luiz took another cold potato,
looked the larger, meaner, uglier boy
straight on and said:

"For stabbing a kid in the face."
The chow line went quiet.
"Then you are stupid, ain't ya,"
the larger, meaner, uglier kid spat,
"watcha go and do that for?"

And Luiz, now lifting an extra sausage,
turned back to the mouthy, horny toad,
and said:
"He said he'd see me later,
only,
I couldn't wait that long."

In Mount Olive (2009)

plucked dead from icebound ocean
lifeless salvage lain to rest
in cold hard earth of halifax
mummified survivors of black april night in 1912
when lights went out & luxury ceased
& a band played "autumn" in darkest spring
amidst screaming throes
women & children first
step from grand lady nosing down
to a bed 12,500 feet below
at 2.20 a.m. roughly positioned at
41 degrees 46' N
fifty degrees 14' W
vanishes ungracefully
& the boatless floating gaffed by dawn
transported to nova scotia
entombed ice sculptures for eternity
in mount olive cemetary.

Daddy's Bad Seeds (2009)

O Yay/O Yay/ now hear this/ my sodly father/the mentally unstable ogre/ patriarch of our family unit/ beast of all he surveyed/ never did take to art/ in any shape or form/ not one bit/ tho/ to his detriment/ he did take a strop/ regularly/ to me/ for childly/sonnish/ bad deeds/ and much as I detest/ loathe the fact/ the man/ strive not to ponder/ what is in/ my jeans and genes/ i know/ I will never/ be rid/ shot of/ spent/ distanced from/ my heathen father's/ duplicit/illicit/bad seeds/ O Yay/ O Yay.

fight club (2009)

i got beaten up @ school once
by a girl called Hilary Zoel
JA ZOEL! they used to call her,
she was tall, athletic,
half-german, all-ayrian,
i ought to have hit
her back @ least once, for
dignities sake, only
i couldn/t as i had
a crush on her. even
after she/d whupped on me,
called me swine, & spat on me.
if Ja Zoel had been in the war,
man, with that much spunk,
the germans might just have won.

life in the slow lane (2009)

@ the atm today, drinking gutrot red ink agen,
sum vain hope of anonymous donation/benefaction,
wishful fiscal vistas, then the slip spewed out,
in black, print only, nonclassified, contrary to my
own damned bottom line, in fact id been transacted
on overnite stock exhanges for pork bellies & gold & dropping crude,
& now i hung out indebted to faceless brokers,
beyond disrepair, deep into gray despair,
of empty financial recklessness insolvent solvent abuse,
of automatic cancellations high up in portfolio constellations,
where IMF weary ex-world bank poets on route to
zonian lives by dead polluted canals,
with yellow handmaids & rusted loins & balconies,
drop shrapnel & coins into wishing wells,
while i stand bereft, means tested, overspent.

Thatz Feminista Mista! (2009)

& freda kahlo didnt cum to my wedding,
too busy with the red people disembarking,
& i never went to my wedding,
tied up with the yellow people boarding,
& the big white whale & Conrad did attend,
i heard, while over at the hollywood bowl
a phosphorous haze hung heavy as
the shaman danced & girls cried openly.

aqua girl (2009)

A brief moment in child time.
I wanted to be gordon. Pilot of thunderbird V.
A puppet sure, but with good moves.
Underwater, performing international rescue duties.
Marina the aqua girl, good-looking kelp in a swishy gown.
    When I got stuck under the breakwater's stanchion –
    there was no mermaid assistance. Only the Sally
    army bugle boy dived in, attired in full regalia,
    saved my life. I almost drowned many times,
                    the liquid life of water signs.

to hear her voice once more (2009)

of course, i believed her dead
lying somewhere slowly decomposing
drug residue seeping from her opened pores
her hair matted with dirt and lavae
her fingers discoloured
her eyes gone to the crows
and i accepted it all, after time
my only mistake, was in deleting her from my phonebook
in case she ever called again

Hard Rock Candy Mountain (2009)

like walking sticks on evergreens deciduous
in celophane that crinkles like compacted snow
sweets they used to weigh for paper bags
now arrive candy coated in brittle light
cracked on teeth hard with poison gas
the sound of resurrection from within
neurotic soft centrered incidents hang motionless
the lingering aftershock taste of absinthe laced
chartreuse on tongues and throats and lips so blue
on a plane high above the steppe and shepherdesses
i recall her taste momentarily, hard rock cafe
breakfasts tainted with psychotic stripes
a subtitled cinema goer from a chocolate box lid, kid

Boys Will Be Boys I Guess (2009)

mostly ...
i strived in earnest to be one,
everyone wanted it,
i got the sore knees, nose picking & dirty hands down pat,
i learned the marbles, the catapault & the bows & arrows too,
then i acquired the knowledge – i smashed things up, stole, lied,
fell out of a tree & off a wall,
& all for nothing ...
i squandered my best days being a boy,
though, it did make people laugh,
happy when they saw me sitting in casualty with a saucepan
    wedged on my head,
mostly ...
that is what they always remember about me,
that bloody saucepan.

If I Should Have To Go To A Family Funeral (2009)

Though probably I won/t be invited.
But if I was, and some decrepit old aunt
reeking of gin, says to me 'And which side of the family are you
    on dear?'
I think I shall say 'None. I'm only an interested bi-stander.'
I think that would be the most perfunctory manner in
which to handle funeral small talk.

I Had Pancakes ... (2009)

in a diner on,
interstate whotever,
with teamsters & whores 4 company,
all doused in syrup,
& i put the boss on the jukebox,
atlantic shitty,
& juliette lewis arrived,
lookin mighty fine,
killed two men, i just laughed,
& sid was dead, tracks & humiliation,
chelsea hotel oblivion,
i went to nyc & it stank,
& iggy played,
no tickets left,
in time square, but rochelle was cheap,
six bucks fifty till day light,
& travis laughed, in death i sleep,
i died 8 times in A-merica.

vacationary tail on woodsmoke (2009)

they left bacon in the fridge, pig, think about it,
& portwine, & a woodheater ready to flare
like i was, like i am, about, fauna of alienation
back among the vines & driftwood & in their bosom
without their realization bar one, invading
watching england dreaming, winning, climbing
fascinated with woodstock, janis, jimi, mud, drugs, guts,
pissin it up, on, & fuckin in daylight darkness in-between
like assassins
like matadors
like predators all, in red, cloaked, death by choking on …
sweet that bake, that bargain trolley, quaint that cafe
paid a bill unrecognized
got lost temporarily
found poe, a condensed volume, in a flea market
imagine that, but couldnt put syllables
together coherently before or after the
pipe of peace
it was bear country
once … & i was bare there
but no more – it is smoke.

the cost of it all (2009)

in quiet moments, behind closed doors, in dark rooms,
i often thought, that one fine day, when i was me, i would
    probably be,
quite the tramp.
    why, i can't say. all this changed however, when i found out
    the true cost of a
non lubricating turned inside-out-pretend-vagina. & when they
    told me, that to reach trampdom, i might well have to spend
    my urinary tract uptime, prostrate in the bathtub.
    this was not how i envisioned things. & why is it, that most
    essentials a woman needs, merely to function day-to-day,
    inevitably come with a high-end price tag attached?
    vaginas, obviously, don't come as cheap as dreams.

YOU ARE NOT A PUNK PUNK (2009)

the only
occasion you could
reach that
epiphany
is if you were
in the can & some
muscle laden
big dick
with a skull & crossbones
tattooed on each
eyelid
made you his
bitch
boy

Serpentine Kiss Of Life (2009)

sisters grimm
lobar as the tide recedes
daylight floods
propylene glycol green
paroxysm ha ha
sea worms bloated on my stomach
the oil beetle grows fat on night markets
questionable tastes
i recuperate post resuscitation

in a cake tin lined with stale imagery
as the nurse stoops glides twitters
betwixt me, it, them and a sea so beautiful no one dare sail it
till dawn.

spanish windlass – (2008)

with each and every calculated twist
        of your love stick
my breathing labours ... shorter, softer
        until finally my whispers can only be heard
by the dead
exhale exhale exhale ...

        & in another dimension i stand aside the charnel pit,
        bird-dogged, staring into the molten black eyes of a
        horny thing and i smile ... inhale inhale inhale

38 Teared Wedding Cake (2009)

shackled conjoined, two
    dumb smiling plasticine figurines
off white
    bejeweled ripped gowns
          nursing shotguns acock
sepia bonnie & bonnie
on the eve of death
beguiling
the weight of our combined guilt opens an icing crevasse where
   glycine drips

   & we two vanish together
forever
entombed in a marzipan underworld of sweet deceit.

THIRD PARTY GROOMING (2008)

salon smells enticing aroma theraputic perfumery
scents, intense incense – soft ambient machines – electrolysis
fellatio
rhythmic stimulation hot wax sensation triple X clean white
mood lite
pluck strip squeeze pore – girls inviting white smiles tender
touches
use abuse cosmetic air brushes make us feel a million bucks

the road to my grave (2008)

is lined on either side by high hedges
amidst which wild bluebells & blackberries tumble
over which are views like a Constable painting
above which are skies where swallows enact an avian battle of
Britain,
beyond which lies our true Camelot, & it is a road
Orwell would have enjoyed rambling down on a
bright English summer's afternoon to find
my grave aside those of Nelson, Keats & Flash Gordon;
saviours of the universe.

REDUX (2008)

The Redux release,
is the fully unexpurgated version,
of your life story.
The version that plays
silently on giant flat screens
as you climb the stairway to heaven

THE HOUSE (2008)

I built a house with my grandfather, day-by-day, month-by-month, brick-by-brick.
My parents then moved into this house and began to tear it, and themselves, apart, day-by-day, month-by-month, year-by-year, piece-by-piece.

One day, when my grandfather and me where building this damned house, he told me we were "Building a mausoleum". It is only now, in later life, with the full clarity of hindsight, that I understand precisely what he meant.

Not long after my grandfather and me built this house, he died sitting upright in his favoutite armchair. At the chapel of rest, for some still unknown reason, they had coloured my grandfather's cheeks with rouge and his casket was lined in pink satin.
I always found this odd. That my grandfather, a man who had de-fused bombs in WWII, and built grand houses for humankind, should meet his maker made up like a cheesy drag queen ...

Girl With A Glass Eye (2008)

The first girl I ever kissed, had a glass eye.
After we'd kissed, she took it out & showed me it.
Then she put it in her mouth & sucked it.
Stuck it back in the socket & asked me if I wanted to kiss her
    again.
Naturally, I declined.
Ever since, I have always thought about her.
Whether she performed that trick with every boy she kissed
    hence,
& whether or not they kissed her again after her party piece.

Laura Lies (2008)

outside my house when I was 14
straddling her bike when she was just 12
sucking her hair/skin raw with cold
weds me mentally before I grow old(er).

1 in 3000 years (2008)

They called it the 1 in 3000 years heatwave.
Praise be I will never experience it again.
There was no big black dog called Harvey,
no Son of Sam rampage,
no white suits, bee gees, mohawks, grease or gay
peek-a-view booths running cold
only a relentless sun of God sauteeing my few remaining
brain cells into a stir-fry submission.
Ladies in hats stood in a tent withering.
A famous feminist orated on matters at hand, then fled.
I crashed my car. The milk curdled. All the taps ran hot.
I lost my mind in the 1 in 3000 years heatwave.

lemon colored grab bag (2005)

on one rosh hashana
i grabbed for her grabbag
while she was entangled
in the philodendrum bush
& hi to her hairline
on novocaine
having spent the entire day
making lemonade
the leitmotif of her life
in crushed citrus rind
not even ironic
she was under no excess duress
as i drew up my cowl
in the watery moonlight
her bucktooth glinted
dear god i thought
i cursed myself & the idiotic satellite
we swapped vasular seconds
her & i
she went slenderized
i went for the barbecue fork
she hit me with the teakettle
i hadnt even heard it whistling
point break

PAM (2008)

empty green bottles
    stale vomit & full ashtrays
      matted oxfam coat hosting flea circus show
        hungover ballerina in yesterday's make up
          lying naked in urine stained bathtub sends me to
            off license
           to beg borrow or shoplift a bottle of something
             to jump start her day
            later: face down in the gutter talking to god
            as a paddy wagon arrives on the scene ...

Strange Girls Who've Been ... (2008)

Some, are like express trains rocketing through
dark tunnels over tracks made from my bones,
others are like the slowly bending exoskeletons
of heaven reaching towers of man. Some are
plasma always in dire need of water; others,
are frugal with natural resources.

Some burn like November the fifth, others just
flicker, candles lacking wick. Some steal my shoes,
use my cosmetics, others get weepy, broody
and wicked. Some of them are very strange,
others, ought never to have left that home out
on the range.

Some talk incessantly. Remind me of smoky bars
on saturday nights in Paddington. Others seem
barely coherent or cognisant, as untouchable as
a bouquet of comfrey. Physical epitaphs on my
own fatality. Some brush their hair so savagely,
the breaking strands make my nerve ends
vibrate. Others, don't hardly run a comb at all.

Some, are intrinsically intrusive. Rummage as
thoroughly as warrant holding narco cops. Others,
are humanity shy, as cold and silent as your own
burial plot. Some bite, lamia's post-lent, others just
lay corpse like, their eyes locked on the ceiling,
cold blooded humanoids devoid of feeling ...
pleasure or pain.

Last Two Eves (2008)

I had a dream
t'other nite
that you & I
were the last
two people left
alive & it was
a beautiful coda
to the madness
& bestiality
that once passed
for humanity.

feral dykes (2004)

gun totin
cone smokin
fish guttin
flanny wearin
hard livin
home brew guzzlin
nest makin
horse ridin
veggie growin
trash talkin
feral dykes

(Teri Louise Kelly vs Recyclopath)

Lulu Mars (2008)

always wore a fulllength rabbitfurcoat
was addicted to sugar cubes
bloodymarys/loureed/me
i accompanied her to
the meth-O-done clinic,
thrice weekly full stop
she pawned the coat
to a greek to buy cigarettes,
gave out bjs free.
I couldnt watch her slap for veins
night after night, while i
watched charlies angels,
so i dumped her at grand
central station locker #261.

the cold bitch from nowhere i knew (2008)

she'd gone
before she'd
even arrived
another vanished
blip on the radar
of the time & space
continu – uhm.
It was odd, but,
not unusual. Simple
logic told me
she'd obviously
received a classier
offer in the interim.

On The Metro En Femme (2008)

dressed in ultra tight leather skirt
black seamed stockings
five inch red stilettos
the old man lowers le monde
surveys me like a purveyer
on the metro i feel french

I Blame It On Midwifery (2008)

that too-hard smack set this life
in motion – locomotion
made me mechanical
prone to rust, inertia, gas
caused the square root sum
of disassociative dissoloution
solitude
on roaring forties, fifties, sixties,
soul survivor drifts by mainstream unnoticed,
looking back on subtle twists and shouts
nuances of murderous decay
advancing stealthily
on human form: mercedes benz
of mammal-dom
bend it any other non-right way
discard it
blood makes too much noise.

Biting (Hot) (2008)

go get me a
tv dinner
a crossdressing hooker
six michelobs
& when you come back
maybe ill bite ya
some more
lil sophomore.

WishBone (2008)

I want to pull her
like a wishbone
snap her
get the Y piece
and wish she
wasnt ever here.

New England Seafood (2008)

Suzee ex TriBeCa gave me crabs but Mary Ann only fed me
shrimp as she talked
incessantly bout Cornish and Holden reclusive F. Scott and
Zelda insane the great neck
shore literary bore and my balls itched so freaking much i
hadda go get lotion while Dahlia
the florist squeezed my hand and told me that New England
was famous for its
scrimshaws seafood ... and screwballs

second sight (2008)

my mother always told me
she possessed the gift of
second sight could foretell
everything id ever do full stop
Well, she never saw
this coming eh?

cherokee (2008)

drivin to westchester nys with
the cherokee (only one sixteen
by the way) lookin for shelter
a place to lie, lay, even love
awhiles. My aunt said sharonne
was just trailer trash (undoubtedly true)
but like, good manners cost nought
irish pat slipped us twenty
we drove to sharonnes cousin in
the bronx (thirteen times removed
from reservations) i told sharonne
after eight days, that the plymouth
was past due. I drove it to jfk
dumped it in long stay – all the
lights in nyc blazed as the big dumb
jumbo banked out over the sound

IAN CURTIS (2008)

dead at 23
hung in semi
detached misery
the abject token
of indecision
unable to choose
between loves
lives, wives.
Lost control.

Flat Chested Girls (2008)

resemble adrogynous young boys/
cropped hair/ blank stares/ baggy
pants/ pill popping ways/ post pubescent
barely legal tender/pimply angst/
non-conforming couldnt careless/ cant say
what it was ever attracted me to them/
once

the girl with the pale green eyes (2008)

telescopic sights hunt me
stalk/terrorize me render
me icarus under caesious sun
god defile pure thoughts
simultaneously snatch snippets
of my soul/rebuild me far less
than the hole languid green
gaze enraptures
shunts mona deep into
venetian haze track my every
move shadows resistance
futile to care/resist all
temptation. still life aquamarine
scene in which I flounder/drown
greet zen master beckoning
exanimate day of incandescent
reckoning *doli incapax* swear
this buddah demands to
chant it LOUDER.

the hourglass upturned (2009)

time cheats everything
bar the exquisite beauty
of a newly interred teenage girl

Show Me (2008)

how you look sporting that big bertha you bought on special
the rhythm method and its intricacies
the soles of your feet the morning after you danced all night
    bare footed
your eyes before and after that mother of all binges
the drugs you keep in that locked cabinet
your laundry hamper on wash day
your tonsils and tongue last thing at night
your ink and appendicectomy scar
your ass imprinted with the pattern of your office chair
the backs of your knees the crooks of your elbows your armpits
    freshly shaved
the back of your neck after the sun has kissed it raw
show me what you fear the most in this life and beyond
what you ingest digest think dream feel touch manipulate
show me around your hood by nightfall tumbleweed
the muzzle of your gun and ill show you the meaning of love

punctate basophilia (2008)

there is obviously too much
lead in your pencil
as under the microscope
my immature red blood
corpuscles are all turning
blue, diagnosis: i am allergic to you.

LIPS (red as a turkey cock) (2004)

dreamed of first kiss
divine full magenta hue
drank wine crimson dark
vinaceous pout becomes her on
this bed bad thoughts inside
my head illuminates
demoniacal desire drives bad thoughts
porporate haze motel stays
rubescent spins my cycle
dusky pink movie star methinks
any colour she paints those
lips sends me on orgasmic trips.

planet areola (2008)

they need to send a wo-mann ed mission
to explore the terrain of
that glandaceous landscape

Mango Body Butter (2008)

when you smeared it all over me
rubbed it into every pore n
crevice with the tender care
of a gourmet marinating wild fowl
i felt like the most exotic ingredient
on a smorgasbord for the duke of death
n it was only after you began
to devour me that i realized that
i was dessert.

Heartland (2009)

there is a desolation in my existence,
one that is, simultaneously,
poignant & inspiring,
one that, in moments of recalcitrance,
jars me to recollect, that I have wrecked,
to achieve the objective,
not one thought, worthy of pursuit,
here, sentiment rarely sprouts,
emotion blossoms irratically,
empathy flowers bi-annually at most,
no matter, I have trained myself,
to embrace desert conditions,
to thrive in an abstract environment,
befriending isolation I become rooted,
a stubborn, unyielding tiara of thorns,
infrequently visited by physical life.

life as it is, in the orchestra pit … (2009)

in other lives, i transgressed, i now confess,
so at the melting point of this old fresh start,
i received exactly my fair dues, no matter the abhorrent
    abberation,
such was, my pennance, my pendant,
destined for one full cycle at least he thought,
to be reminded each and every time the mirror and i met,
that in this human incarnation, i should reflect back at
myself when naked as the day i was still born,
a little pink and wrinkled baby elephant's head.

Camille Carcrash (2009)

She always preached that if you yanked enough pricks, one day
    you'd hit the jackpot & find a good man who shat gold.
        Which was how, she came to be coming around the
hairpin with her eyes blazing, her belly swollen, her pussy
sodden, after interfacing with another human slot machine
that only spewed up evens.
        It explains why her vision was impaired, her
judgement flawed, her mind a perfect square, & why, above
all else – she stank.
        Obviously, the tree saw her before she saw it & the
tree never flinched & to her credit, neither did she.
        They put dead flowers there some time later, to X
the stain where another moonbeam got extinguished on
an ordinary wretched day while someone else hit paydirt
someplace else. Kerching.

extempore – right now (2009)

i am trashed – again
i am to blame – again
i lack rectitude
& yet i was clean last nite
& the nightmares came, a prowlin
& i got fucked up – again
lost my mind my courage my fortitude in a glass, no, eight
listenin to the hilltop hoods
babblin shit eatin cold rice i think im dead
my bed is icy like my grave
i dont wanna die in there i wanna pass to red in a bar
drinkin my thirteenth coronary cocktail
scribblin lines on napkins
eatin mixed salted nuts
spellin the word intoxicated mentally
while decent folk go about righteous business
bombing religions that aint mine
& i can screw & piss & shit & fuck & lust
aerobic capacity remains
as mental alacrity diminishes
they sell me amyl nitrate cut with ajax
debase the disease i acquired one hundred years ago in that
    place
& if i had to choose id tick lethal injection over electrocution

girls like me (2008)

get to die every day
get spat at shat on
jeered & ridiculed
for daring to be
alive. girls like me
in this world full of hypocricy
pimp their own buns
in red light districts
just to make it to
the promised
land. girls like me get
to ride all the rides
for twice the recommended retail price.

INKED (2008)

every single nerve ending in my body rests unaware
that within seconds, i will be cut.
Even as it's happening, my central nervous system
refuses to accept the obvious.
For the first few moments, I feel nothing but
exhilaration. A rush, that i'm being cut by design,
a buzz that i'm sitting there, sucking in the
cloying atmosphere of antiseptic air.
Delayed reaction, white blood cell stampede,
bottlenecking to the scene of my self-inflicted
crime, arrive too late and the pain
is so intense i'm biting through my
own tongue. I am being inked, marked for
all eternity so that on the days i don't feel alive,
i can look at the telltale stamp and remind
myself, that once in a while, I truly was.

tag team piercing (2008)

i went with a rock star
to get my nipple pierced
& she went first
because she was more famous
more desecrated
wilder
& when she screamed
oh fuck
as the needle slid through
her brown nipple
i nearly pissed my pants
with apprehension
then i sat there
& through it went, clean,
more painful than love
or hate or orthodontry
& i screamed jesus
though i still didnt find
theology on jetty road.

Red Phone Boxes (2009)

like in dr who,
like on carnaby street,
& when i ever needed to make a call –
to my mother reverse charges,
to my probation officer reverse charges,
or to confess to the Samaritans something i hadn/t yet, but
    might, still do/ne,
there was always a red phone box somewhere that smelled of:
piss, shit, vomit, ale, tobacco, lust, death, fear, obsession, night,
    righteousness,
i need to go to a red phone box someplace remote once more,
& dial the voice that gives you the time, or,
the weather; & feel connected again to westminster.

die verkürzte Version meines Lebens (in fucking english)

ein zwei drei vier ...
my mother was lady fucking godiva & my
father was isambard kingdom brunel
we lived on a shabby council estate
where the post-war boom hadn/t fucking
arrived & where everyone said fucking
a fucking lot

i had to go to school to learn violence,
to learn how to fight,
to learn who to fight,
to learn when to fight,
to fight about fucking fighting
& to fight for my right to fucking fight

i got arrested for fighting
& elizabeth regina/ who it was said
ruled over me, gave me detention at her
fucking pleasure; shaved my head, washed me
with a fire hose, & then made me fight
small bears naked for her fucking entertainment

by the time i was ready, willing & able
to fight, there was no fucking war. war was over & out,
dope smoking japanese women posing
naked were in, so, with no war to
die heroically, or fucking cowardly in,
we could only fight or up fuck each other.

they taught us to fight so fucking well,
that they couldn/t stop us, then, they
called us scum & fucking hooligans & set
alsations on us: no one called them
german shepherds, because after all –
we had won the fuck fuck fucking war
die fuck fuck fucking krieg
1-2-3-4 ...

Abridged rejection letter from the editor of a
prestigious US poetry journal (2009)

dear madam (question mark)
thank for your latest submission to blah blah
firstly, let me congratulate you on succeeding in taking the genre
to new & somewhat disconcerting lows,
& while i feel sure that in this day & age work such as this would
    find
a willing, albeit, uneducated audience, i must also add that in part,
your work demonstrates the true spirit of maladjustment

in response to your query as to whether Ezra Pound is still on the
submissions board, i reply that he most certainly is, in spirit.
As you are no doubt aware, blah blah, has a reputation
for traditional, inspiring verse, penned by some of the nations
leading literary pens. That work, which you will have seen had you
taken the time to perhaps peruse a past issue,
does not in whole or part, contextualize vaginoplasty,
pedastry
nazi war criminals
bestiality
whether or not hemingway had a homosexual crush on a bullfighter,
intravenous narcotics use,
the unabomber's manifesto in eight verses,
breast augmentation for eunuchs,
john wayne gacy
anal intercourse,
japanese pornography,
et al

i do feel that your work, profound as it is,
would be far better suited to
a publication with a keen sense of indecency –
access to adequate legal counseling,
& editors with a stronger constitution for the bizarre

yours etcetera

Lester Bangs, Baby ... (2009)

didnt read him till too late,
tied up with Buks, Yates & the fly fisherman bent,
tho when i did i saw the angle, his slanted take,
on music dead & dinosaurs gone,
he was always in, they said, but in but out if you catch my drift,
whereas i am always in but out but out, some simularity there,
was the truth too painful, too fixating,
that inside music tied in bars & chords,
lester just plain forgot bout other words, & longer forms,
& died a good death – a rockish exit,
& lester banged, i think he did,
with china cymbal cysts on pulpy eyelids,
staggered haggard up to rolling stone.

meantime ever never (2008)

no navigator could plot by stars –
longtitude and latitude the intercourse of our desires,
for even if we two could, somehow copulate once
again – anally, vaginally, orally, anyoldally, the
mathematical sum is certifiably less than its coagulated
     anatomical parts.

we will never be found locked together like ornate
victorian garden statues always at it on kew,
our love, alas, is destined to lie fallow, to be as
lifeless, as mortis, as a thousand year old mummy
spreadeagled on the meridian line, so i ask
you one last time for posterity; when will you ever grasp the
     finality of failure?

when will you repunzelize the facts? of this matter –
dearest darling heartbreaker, awaken from
your technicolour dream and see our corrosive world of
lies and promises moulded with disease, see our lust
maggot infested – open your fucking eyes and see
that while you slept i quit being your oracle and opened my
     soul to the meantime.

My Devil Could Be Yours (2008)

eat my flesh,
suck out my tongue,
the marrow of my
stewed bones,
ingest my spirit,
stiffle my screams,
asphyxiate my hate,
extinguish my flame,
ride me to hell and back
on the nighttrain,
rip my heart into bite size pieces,
embrace my inner demon,
betrothed as the pit gapes like syphiloma
and my devil becomes yours to
have and to caress through all
damnation ...

the only boy i ever loved (2009)

Lived the hermit life on an istmus that jutted out into a vivid
pink viscous ocean
where his blue eyes bewitched the light, my intransient
transendental wayfarer,
marooned like a ship in a bottle on a dusty mantelpiece.

Under the satinwood trees we'd meet, my boy and me, just
shooting the breeze, two composite characters adrift on the
stage in the theatre of the absurd,
there I left him red-headed and freckled, my own private
castaway.

Penile Penal Colony (2008)

se men deposit in safety boxes
at sperm banks where non-interest
bearing is guaranteed & discretion
& privacy rests assured to be
harvested by housewives tilling
infertile plains & barren dykes
two-up on bikes all hasting and
basting to catch bullet trains
passbooks withdrawals at the
investment penile colony of man.

DeAd Set JeNnY (2008)

no one said a word when i pushed her into the pond
they were all too busy guzzling gin slings
she only blew bubbles as i held her under
watching and waiting to be disengaged
they started guffawing over dogs and bitches
so i let her up and she ran screaming inside
while i just sat there and wondered why
she hadnt even tried to oblige us and die.

not quite venice beach (2009)

80 somethin, im a new pale face,
wanderin round the bay, by day & by night,
especially by night, @ lennies, where the big hair
spray pumped to poison & jon bon j,
drinkin beer from stubbies, wine from bladdas,
drownin most days,
in hospital with 3rd degree burns,
learnin greek/ language of TAB/ antipodean hookers
getting universitied
fryin my mind, runnin away west with underage flesh
in the backs of panel vans, cruisin the
papier mache mountain for same,
watchin the virgin olive oil boys pump lead in the cage,
rolla bladers with walkmans, fake traders,
dealers, hawkers, stalkers, but all of this was b4:

> gentrification
> dry zones
> oysta bars
> sand dredging
> skin cancer
> search & seize
> oprah
> upskirtin
> wars on drugs/terror/indivuality/speech
> DNA
> patriotism
> pepper spray
> pandemic paranoia ...
> autoerotic asphyxiation kick
> WMDs
> progress yeah

& it wasnt venice beach, not even 4 one thirty 2nd
but i liked it by day & by night,
especially by night.

made in england (2008)

i was handmade in england behind an aircraft hangar
on pasturised english airfield where spitfires and
hurricanes once departed to engage the hun
whose pilots sometimes returned and took liberties
with girls like my mum who in turn gave birth
to a new war effort divided by class all tending
patiently englands green grass from foreign invaders

tAkiNg iT lIkE a MaN (2009)

i have always so admired
your inherent ability to straddle it/
standing up – as you crash head first
down the autobahn of our life
seemingly impervious to pain
laughing at lady death
hands in the air lawless child
though i myself have never
craved it that way as it would
invalidate my life and void
my insurance for sure but
hell i still admire your balls baby

GBH (2009)

primal scream
rebel yell
the underground is cold & dark at 2 a.m. on a friday morning
    ...
they look at you
you can only smell them
then they can smell you too

they all have dead eyes
long black coats
the look of grievous bodily harm personified for a street
    dictionary
& there are no fuzz to be found,
no transport police
& no fucking transportation,
i'm thinking circle

it smells like infirmary,
but i don't move because im frozen to my spot
like that statue of the thinker
up above

they never call you boy
like the song says
they always address you in the feminine pronoun & they call
    you
cunt,
watcha lookin at, cunt,
& they dont move & you dont move & the sum of all the
    parts is somehow way less than the fucking hole youve dug
    yourself into ...
smiling does not work,
fuck the gap & the gold rail
im thinking suicide,

watcha lookin at
pussy
they stick to the feminine address
i stand my ground
im thinking there are 91 steps up because
the escaltion device aint
workin

& they look right
& i look right

& i bolt man i bolt in the masculine present
because i can take 91 steps faster than those cunts can take me.

thermal draughts (2008)

"Who are all these blackclad imposters you asked
pragmatically while you gnawed on sanders skull wasnt it us
after all who soared by the wings of pestilence like yin and
yang locusts cut from the plague who drank clots with vlad
for far higher stakes and read cowleys lemonjuice texts by
candlelight as the draughts swung asymmetrically away while
the pieces shifted by forces unknown interchangeable gutless
pawns and wasnt it us who watched artaud disinterestedly
but the inquisition was laughable the decapitation towering
the dark ages illuminating though the lizard kings tricks did
grow contrite and those toy vamyres had no bite and didnt
you swear youd taken polaroids that theyd been negatively
indecently exposed as the rivers boiled and our blood pooled a
lake where tormented souls of homogenized brood bodysurfed
breakers that died before they even embraced the scorched
desert shore and i remember now we laughed drunkenly at
the intangible touch of distant mortality and you cut a cross
into my skin and it never even bled and we danced till forever
around a bonfyre of lust as hey zeus freaks shrieked in casket
shaped bumper cars and on the mountaintop the wiccagirl
burned in a cage of her own design so hold me closer now
the hour to take confessions draws near and the spiked walls
enclose hungry to leech our ghosts i tell you now i have never
felt this well black hearted eternia"

all the things i left behind voluntarily (2008)

MASTURBATION.
FRUSTRATION.
CONTAMINATION.
INTERROGATION.

DOMESTICITY.
HUSBANDRY.
PATERNITY.
SERVILITY.
BRUTALITY.
FUTILITY.
FERTILITY.

INTERRMENT.
SARCASM.
ORGASM.
TIES.
LIES.
MEMORIES.

all that remains of yester day (2008)

is a carapace
of turquoise
trimmed in gold leaf
a memento of past lives
melting under the blazing aztec sun

Going Underground Part IV (2009)

discombobulated fruitcake
you will soon enough
be underground where
incandescent worms will
hear your confessions
like a mute audience
of idiot savants

Boi Bitch w Morning Tongue (2009)

the first thing i feel every morning
is the abrasive tongue of my boi bitch lover
forcing its way between my own dry lips
pre listerine rinse she wants to orally
molest me and suck my gums clean

Chaud Freud (2009)

my professional diagnosis of the subject
is that this individual suffers from malignant narcissism
deep rooted sexual inadequacies
and a terminal inferiority complex
all over and above a misogynist viewpoint

Like Cobain, Like H. Like Doc (2008)

so friend, it is about four, glass a quarter full, mind raging,
    groin mute, everything popping,
                & you no doubt, sleep,
                right now i see the parallel, the juxt of
cold gun metal pressed against human head.
                listen, i understand.

it is a game, us, me, versus the world & its stupid morality,
    conformity, neccessity (is that spelt right amigo?)
                the insatiable quest of:
                same
                stuck track
                non-skipping vertebrae

& i see the final solution with glass-bottomed clarity magnified,
    that wild card in the DECK.

                it looks like the joker
                ergo, it must be oui?

& i think that you compadre, will see, allegorically, that when
    all else fails; as it undoubtedly will, there is always that door
    marked

                EXIT i can step through

get rejoined, re-wired, made straight, in the factory man,
    because i tell you now, i am getting old/tired/wasted of/with
    all this heartless, soul-less, crap, you call life ...

                        & what are we, in the end
                        & who are you
                        to tell me,
                        one day,
                        they will regret.

A WRITER'S IMAGINATION INVACUO (2008)

& when i'm marooned alone i sometimes think bad thoughts about what she's actually doing 'out there' in the world of undoing.

& when i'm isolated invacuo i do sometimes squander my creative energy drinking & dancing & generally forgetting the state of dual nation.

& when i'm cast away on an atoll of coral i do sometimes feel the pressing need to cut myself to confirm that i haven't yet passed & gone to cyberpunk plain.

& when i'm cryo sealed in a boil in the bag bubble i do fess that my writer's imagination festers & troubles elocutes electrically.

& when i'm stranded on the side of our arterial road i confess that i do sometimes indulge in flatulent conspiracies & consider my life the san andreas fault – ready to open & swallow a declaration of independence.

jet black cocktail (2009)

two thirty amen/this new demographic of lost/unkissed by
    sunlight/outcasts/misfits/rogue traders/outlaw writers ...
                      huddled over screens
                      streets quiet
                      drones and bees zzzzz

daytona tells me she only feels alive @ now, lady zombie
    communes with the undead in subways, loveless remains
    just so by choice,
                      i take their drugs
                      their confessions
                      their night souls

the strawberry stalker rarely calls, catwoman purrs down the
    mainline, white fang hunts spiders, ghoulicious bugs out
    on b-grade, hannah barbarian slays creeps in virtuality, the
    world's greatest author tells me i'm full of shit – and then
    sum ...

                      new legion
                      word creatures
                      dark side
                      reach me on channel 101

miss reign of terror rarely rises before four.

NO CESSATION OF (2008)

i see consequences
periodically comma'd
i see you standing there
dewy-eyed crying inside
clawing at walls
scavaging empty cupboards
watching death in vivid hues
tying my life up in a bow
putting it under your synthetic
christ-mass tree
these are not consequences
these are actions
movements
tempo like checkers
by telepathy
in a bar your car
no one else comprehends
the consequences
of senility or
servility

U KNOW (2009)

u know how it is right?
How it feels when youve
given all u can give
said all u can say
lied all u can lie
fessed all u can fess
written all u can write
begged all u can beg
thought all u can think
drunk all u can drink
eaten all the crap u can stomach
how that feels write down in the
pit of your gut, at the front of
your forehead, deep in the groin,
when everything screams ENOUGH!
U know how that feels right?
How it feels knowing u cant
face one more minute hour day week month year
of that kind of shit
how it feels when u wake up facing the
brutal reality that the total cost at lifes
checkout is beyond your resources and
that despite what they preach, life isnt
even an evens game ... u know how that feels
dont you?

Slippery When Wet (2009)

After all that hype,
turned out my heart was nothing more,
than a thirsty red muscle.
My users manual obsolete,
the nervous system mechanical,
vital signs flatlined.
White-coated mechanics huddle around,
compounded indian-rubber svengalis
bending to my will.
Idempotent, redolent – swaying
    like skinny grey arms on the tree of life in slow commotion,
    miming impoverished applause
as my precious fluid drips incessantly
onto a sistine floor.

(Teri Louise Kelly vs Amelia Walker)

septic hershes kisses (2009)

candy neurosis
wont u pleese please me tonite
at yours
or mine
or betwixt the craic

a chocolatte fix
latex lips
slip that digit up my ass
like licorice

a sherbet dab
tantilizingly tzarish,
in bizarre bedouin tents
like loincloths plus jumping fleas
& psychadelic piranah fish

i can cum 108 times
in my headspace,
on 8 track
reel-2-real
with marilyn
jane
peggy sue
rachel & you goosebumps

an ejaculatory theorum deduced.

That Painful Summertime Last (1980)

The Captain & The Kid fooled around with brown dirt.
Incessant chatter of armies, provos, night patrols in emerald.
A BB gun to shoot rats, kids, birds, bus stop signs.
Delinquency mooning as it laughed & played eternally.

Blue sky everywhere the advent of freedom taken.
New old death, self-destruction, innocence wanton violated.
Destroying shit for no good reason than fury.
Summer blended blood red, a cyclops fell at the fayre.

Warm flat beer from old men's cupboards in Newcastle.
A hay loft, ablaze, the cornfield swayed & withered.
Curling smoke, upwards, eyes always shut to reality.
In the colony upside down, a new seed germinated destiny.

One boy drowned lethargically. One boy met god on the
other side of a shattered car windscreen. One boy simply
vanished forever. In that painful, beautiful, lost summer of
adolesence, we died every day for false hope & greater glory.

superfluous to all extents (2009)

a good son rocks the cradle before taking his
suicide mission to the tower of babel,
while a woman wails – beats steam pit earth
with raw broken hands, anguishes in vain
languishes in this valley of broken dolls

this eden of mind-fucked tourists
where mercantile savants sport
blue-blood-stained garottes and mothers
finger wind-up toys with fathers nesting nearby
placating the semantics of swollen glands.

wallowing in sweet heat, muddied and loose,
stooping before the altars of recognition,
overhead vapour trails scar ultramarine en route
to defile puppet prophets of doom.
woman sighs across the mire as man

consecrates his gender: cauterizes
their place in the sect of metabolism
with a spit ... stains homogenous innocence.
poisons her manhood with shooting stars
hand maid in sacked babylonian harems,
theatrics of violence a staged violation –

blooms brilliantly superfluous to all extents.

(Teri Louise Kelly vs Jenny Toune)

wot was inside my head (2009)

the tech said he saw
more
more skitzofrenia
bestialty
pseudopresentiment
psycho
sis
non consciousness
occult oedipus
decussion
refractive errors
mediacy
fugue
anal retention
unanschaulich
submissive aggressive rejections ...

      in my head,

      & the last time he'd seen so much
      vile, it was in a jar, not long
      after it'd been scooped outta
      albert fish.

The Last Time I Saw Myself Alive (2008)

was the day Penny turned up
in the sports car
with the top down
& she had legs
that reached through space & time
& light & misery & the
only boy who ever really
loved her was me
& i was too fucking
young to do anything about it & she drove
away on sunday after a row
with my mother
& i never saw her again
& even though i was only 10
& she was 32 i was so
certain that one day
i'd catch her up
but i never did
& that was the
last time i can
remember being
alive.

immorality now (2009)

blow me up and hang me in a gallery
i would be the nude in the ruben's room.
feel my libido being smeared across a
pallette of indecencies, make me a
water coloured harlot for dante to admire.
source my oils from exotic places,
paint my pecadillos down to the creases,
stroke, lick, breathe me a heartbeat
in a body that has no boundaries.
Drip my desire onto pre raphaelite men
then wipe me clean with a turpentine rag.
decorate your cube with a spattered vulgarity,
it will be worth it.

i am the pouting anti madonna with
forever moist and pouting lips, the nihlistic
exhibitionist, drawn & stretched taut.
it isn't a matter of distance, or perspective,
on display with the pointed arrow lust of
a thousand horny demons, or my liberty
stained over canvas sheets, it's in the hues
of my contours done justice for flesh junkies
to admire and fingerpaint into wet dreams. it's in the
rampant ambiguity between my legs that makes
the leap from decorum to depravity, it's in
the subtle shade of knowing that however deep the
dive my eyes will follow.

(Teri Louise Kelly vs Kerryn Tredrea)

flagellation by design (2009)

you ought to be available by prescription,
so that i can take you three times daily,
get you on repeats & have you filled,
a pharmaceutical remedy for love malaria
& all air borne viral infections of the
arterial network, where my white walls
crash & your red count soars on the
typhoon of lust, that wreaks havoc on me,
on you, on us, as the capital falls & the
tests all return positive negative, like
interbred spores crusading on horseback,
& the cold crimson light floods my mind,
my eyes, my mouth, & i see you there,
shallow & deep, a hand carved effigy
of my new fallibility & the whole of kind
no longer notices how fragile i am,
as ornate & breakable as a faberge egg.

only the light burns no more (2009)

        those lights of a thousand distant moons,
    wayfarer's headlights of impending doom, reach me still,
    then die on arrival, D.O.A in my emergency room,

        pagan beacons doused by wrath and humility of an
entire race run by
pygmies high on red acid drops, with flaming torches held aloft
    on goat strewn mountainsides,

and the light, your beacon, those lights, city lights, night lights,
    don't reach me no more, comet trail away into total pitch,
    as herdsmen with tribal cultures chant hymns to aerial gods
    and fevered swine,

all evaporate heavenly
the discourse of banality
the gibberish of primate man
and I swear on your book that the light doesn't reach me no
    more,
that it doesn't burn phosphorous
no more
no more.

The Tree House (2009)

lost in the asian triangle
where couples walk hand-in-hand
holding white plastic bags
then watch game shows
on big screen tvs.
where exotic tastes
waft aroma therapy from sizzling pans
& the air is spicy & foreign
like distant tongues,
i chain my bike to hers;
two inanimate objects,
locked in tandem
motionless
while high above
in the canopy of bare limbs,
we take custody
of human forms
& joint & severed interests:
then by light,
pedal to places
where leaves blow into rounds
like decomposing funeral pyres.

MOTHWOMAN PROPHECY (2009)

i am fucking the flying scotsman,
under a cloak of masquerade
scarlett O', short on real time
to dwell, linger, watch the first
pink bit slit, spread into another gay day,
all these diary entries
are exits in waiting
timed, on cue, in a queue, lined-up
like pieces of the internal combustion engine;
rarely still, in locomotion,
a go-go-go dancer
movin on to
appointments
book depositories
dance hall days
grassy knolls
organic aisles
puncture repair merchants
float tanks
assigned assignations of every kind,
i sit & ponder the split personalities
appertaining to
the day dead phantom of the night shagging opera
& i guess i am failing the
acid test.

slip knot love shot/s (2008)

yellow water raft down
my urinary tract
dam my rapids with your skitzo-frenetik DNA
call me collect STI
give me that bitch of a virus,
your saliva running in rivulets
your juices in shot glasses
my desire the chaser
to the codeine hook
you slug one, i slug one,
until the subconscious wanes
& the conscience growls gutteral
& i see your retinas
bloodshot & mainlined in my crosshairs
in the chasm of fragility we bind,
to receptors & raptors of our kind
copulate in mammaldom:
you lode me full of spores
i flood you full of vagrant
co-dependency;
your organ & my organ
under the big top
mosh pitting to tribal chants
on a 3-tiered day
lie-ing like dogs.

ahab rehab (2009)

i wanna feel you inside of me
no turning back
i wanna feel you clawing at me
biting me, devouring me
no turning back
you fuel my awareness
heighten my animal
take me on journeys to
unknown parallels
smother me in licentiousness
eat me alive, absorb me
no turning back
i wanna feel you next to me
every night
every phase of the moon
every pulse of my 2-stroke
no turning back
cancerian jonah meets
piscean whale
open your mouth
let me enter within
at my own peril.

(To Red)

LEXICANA (2009)

when the muzaks over
& shes turned off the lights
i wake up in the lovejail
from where no contact is available
as the ex goes on a packaged boycation
                          bigtime baby
ive got the mother of all bangovers
like a defacto brat-ass in 'im-so-over-the-freakin-rainbow-sista'
                          & the claw cometh
                          regularly
                          but sweetly
when im under friendly fire,
& true i dont dig lesbimen
nor broads who sport femmestaches,
or otherfuckas
or god forbid
star struck limp-dicked dirty mouthed tranny hoppas
& sumtimes yeah,
        we top it from the bottom up,
        & we dont subscribe to the kunt-a-view
        of the whatever-the-fuck-i-want-gomys,
as we engage in textual intercourse during
lunchbreaks & all leg & off breaks ...
                          consentually,
then we do it for real & do it agen amen,
& she digs me & i dig her & we climb lipstick
mountains using the by-the-hour femmsherpa
                          & dont call us as we're
off the hook baby.

chocolate momma (2009)

henry lee always complained
that his momma made him
dress like a bitch

i say lucky you henry lee,
fuck,
if my momma had done that
i would never have put
chocolate on my dick &
made the dog lick it off,

no ma'am
henry lee was blessed
havin a momma
who could see

        exactly what he needed.

& so i lied twice big deal (2009)

    when the boy
    got knocked
    down by
    the car
    i never
    even cried
    instead i just
    ran home
    & lied

The Liquid Life Of Artists (2009)

Art, she said, is above & beyond all else.
    I considered the statement while she flung dirty underwear
    into a suitcase. Maybe she was right, anyhow.

When she took to hard drugs, lavish promiscuity & Miller's
    lost weekends with libertines, she put it down to art.
    I kept that thought in a bell jar. Along with all the other
    scrappits of random nonsense I had collected like used
    postage stamps.

Then she left no forwarding address. Sent me a postcard
    sometime later with Lautrec in Toulouse on it. I remembered
    that his name was Henri too.
    She went way way down, subterranean, & far far out:
    Enterprising. Wrote later that she had hit a Homer, escaped
    the Iliad; she reminded me of Joyce, only with bigger tits
    and a better ass.

In the end, I stayed resilient. Made art. Thought that maybe
    one day I would Mailer a postcard back, poste resante. It
    would be a portrait of the artist as a dumb fool – swimming
    buck naked in Pollock's aquarium.
    Nevermind.

DIE NACHT BABIES (2009)

die nacht babies scratch at my doors and windows,
desperate to break and enter my diocese of disease
clutching endoscopes and feeding bottles,
vital to study my lymphatic system down
they weep and moan and jabber,
too close to my sacristy – panhandling plasma transfusions for
    membranes,
and advanced technology in lumbar puncture procedures
i ask quietly 'was wird das kosten?'
but they answer only in sign,
with watery hands miming the universal language of love,
and before daylight seeps, i hear them dragging
their instruments of examination away,
into the fading fetid half night.

Full Mental Jacket (2009)

a thousand years more of forced invasion has led me to here,
recently paroled from the animal pharm, wearing nothing but
a syllabilic ammunition belt – gazing at the highwire made of
human sinew & lust that spans the gulf between your cradle
& my grave – wondering if behind those asylum gates on that
far side, opportunity lies or dies like a phantom pregnancy
of counterfeit symbiotic pangs – as high above pterodactyls
    glide
& the intention is lost on an otiose current of discontent –
& i take the first step – toward your inner sanctum where all
things flourish & all things wither – where the human
    condition
is ritually sacrificed to obtuse sun gods & avaricious moon
    children
& the span of the bridge between us is nothing more
than a pirouette of chance ...

low brow poets in serials (2009)

aw fuck
please no
no more of ya low-fi
lyrical die-horreah

cut me some slack, jack
disembark the fucking differential
& riding those straight lines baby

left handed on the curvilinear
some didactic
perverse verse
sexual crim-in-al
blood & bones anew again,

betty paige in danger girl,
mephistophelian brands
& the heads of oh so pretty girls
all in a row
on stakes.

australian blow job (2009)

where the streets cross/
vanish into bitumen fondue/
she shines a little light/
onto spurious lives/

smelling of onion rings/
doused in fake kylie scent/
orthodontistry abandoned/

deadstopping traffic/
& deadheads/
en route to & from/
the bottle shop.

yesterday was sunday (2009)

strange times
new people
old people
celebrations
a tower of sugar buns melting
return of manga vegans
one new vego
a dyke a byke a cayt
exes
everywhere
miss communication
versus
miss understood
aluminium rails for my little ponies
dilation
ammunition wet
fades to matte gray
fuzzy.

the curious case of you (2009)

I footfaulted poe
then doyle,
hardly rocket science
as methodically I
eliminated the milieu
of possibilities & happenstance
until all that remained
residual
no matter how illogical,
somehow resembled
the truth of your
mysterious
disappearing act.

the time i met yeats in kensington (2009)

w.b had just walked outta of the irish club
onto kensington high street
heading for the book depository,
looking like he'd just come
from the chelsea registry office,
which was after all, only a jig away
& the confetti was trailing in his wake –
anyhows

i knew his housekeeper claudette
was due to marry wordsworth
news spread on the backs of rats,
yeats didn't look so happy,
cruising well over the legal speed limit
sporting a yellow carnation

in the store, i caught him fingering celine
rather disinterestedly,
heard blitzkrieg bop in his headphones,
saw his shades were gold rimmed
& that his beard was apocalyptic –
theologian esque;
yeats looked like fucking god,
the morning after ...

i had intended, in the instant,
to maybe grab his autograph,
get him to sign my jane austin biography
then thought better of it when that
brute shelley crashed in waving a
fistful of atheistic pamphlets,
shouting that god was for half wits & poetry for full ones.

miss tides of march (2009)

the crabs migrate
capitulate
under hermaphrodite carapaces
crustaceans on parade

in piscatorial waters
she hunts languidly
for a mate
to spawn aquatic
to devour
to crush ... to roe egg laden,

as the levels rise
& the fever of the dance increases
in tempo & rhythm
& submerged latin riffs,

she curls her wet body around me
& flexes mussels
& dorsal fins
showing eight rows of teeth
all the better
to rip me with,

i go sideways in fear
navigating undulating longitude
& latitudean nudes
where sterner creatures than i
inside of mammals
down at 20,000 leagues
have already
gone
never to return to surfaceworld,

i will drown down there
in the black
looking at dilated fish eyes
giant goddess squid
& indecent proposals

THE DAY I MET GOD FOUR TIMES (2009)

I. 10 a.m. (on the toilet) – Promulgating.

    all the lights came on; not only in Memphis.
    my bathroom resembled the Tropicana in Las Vegas.
    god arrived, with a theatrical whoosh of his cape.
    slicked back his hair with bejewelled fingers.
    asked me howinthahell i was doing, man.
    i said, fine. couldn't think of anything else.
    god was wearing blue suede shoes.
    told me to shake my ass; he needed the can bad.
    i obliged, naturally, god said: thank ya very much.

II. Midday (in the cafeteria) – Percolating.

    all the lights went out,
    the whole placed smelled like cordite,
    i was eating a tuna on wholemeal sandwich,
    god sat opposite me, he looked brow-beaten,
    &, half of his head was missing.
    god asked me, how far to the knoll?
    i looked bemused, dazzled,
    god got up, made to leave, straightened his tie,
    told me not to ask what he could do for me,
    but instead, what i could do for him.

III. 4 p.m. (asleep at my desk) – Procrastinating.

    i remember feeling giddily spatial.
    aware of my loss of gravitational interference.
    i was floating up, into the ether ...
    god affixed his umbilical cord to my docking port,
    i couldn't see his face, god was an astro-nought,
    he gestured toward something, earth, maybe,
    god & me took one small step for man,
    &, one giant leap for mankind ...
on the dark side of the moon.

IV. Midnight (cowboying) – Pacifistic.

    radical man, groovy, i heard god say,
    i turned over, god was aside me, sporting a full beard,
    god said it had been a hard day's night,
    i said, right on, imagine that,
    god said he was a working class hero, &, proud to be,
    i said, good, man,
    god said he was bigger than god,
    &, that peace had no real chance,
    i said: look man, i've got to get some sleep, okay?
    god said: fab, love love me do.

Lost in space (2009)

half finished glasses of wine,
a pipe,
dvd on pause
a trail of garmentual evidence

leading to the timescene
discarded bras
hers & hers ...

one mad dash
to another dimension
where penetration
stimulates high end sensation

& it never stops orbiting
the circle of entanglement
fuelled by carcinogens
& duologue

we backtrack through the night
by light
collecting the memories
from where they fell to earth
decently incidently.

THE LIBERTINE (END) (2009)

DO

      YOU

            LIKE

                  ME

              NOW?

L.U.S.T (2009)

crazy for IT,
this is a one-way highway
to reckless abandonment
of principles held
by higher gods

i know you're there,
i smell your womanhood
dripping
onto my manuscript,
as i bathe in the rhetoric
of infidels

we swim in rips
at & below sea level,
two incarnate mermaidians
on the tide of contact sport;
beached & sun-dried
resexualization.

Teri Louise Kelly
Adelaide, South Australia
2009

atta-girl@hotmail.com

Available for Pagan Weddings, Eulogies, Pig Spit BBQs &
Unlicensed Psycho-Analysis

Wakefield Press is an independent publishing and
distribution company based in Adelaide, South Australia.
We love good stories and publish beautiful books.
To see our full range of titles, please visit our website at
www.wakefieldpress.com.au.